Copyright © 2021 High Priestesses of Poetry. All rights reserved.

Poems copyright their respective authors.

Copy editing by Andra Vltavín.

ISBN 978-1-7338246-8-2

HIGHPRIESTESSES.COM

HIGH PRIESTESSES of POETRY

an anthology

2020

VOLUME THREE

SAMANTHA CIMINO

BIRCH DWYER

ASH GOOD

GABBY HANCHER

JENN LALIME

SIERRA VIDA LISA

HOLADAY MASON

BETH MELNICK

DAWN THOMPSON

LUNITA VALERIA VELÁSQUEZ

ANDRA VLTAVÍN

AHUVA S. ZASLAVSKY

♦

Origin

HIGH PRIESTESSES OF POETRY arrived in a vision—
12 poets who gather on the eves of each solstice & equinox
to co-create potent thresholds for nonmaterial osmosis.

Worldly experiences are pulled in as seed & digested. Our stories
unfurl in inner sanctuary to grow communal intimacy, feed individual
craft & breathe meaning back into our outer lives.

You may notice the edges of our voices blur into one anothers'
in the muses who feel their way through this temple of word—
affirming that, in the hallways of others' stories, we find mysterious
doorways to our own.

May this sharing of our playful companionship—another
volume of our circle's poems—point you toward the power &
possibility of feeling your way (even in the dark), of laying
claim to your own utopias, of finding your people.

Preface

IT'S ONLY EXCITING to live through the first days of unprecedented times. Months into the plague we realize train wrecks happen in slow motion. There—*there we are!*—hovering midair & contorted, one arm outstretched for ground that may be years away. Our spine has never bent like this & no wonder we are tender.

How is your heart? a priestess may ask. This is not a question you can hide from. How *are* our hearts? It is not easy. At this point we are tired of letting our noses itch until we can get home to wash our hands. All this holding space is hard—these 6 feet bubbles that must bloom out, learning to veer off course for safe passing, how we can touch a leaf but not hold hands. We are tired of Brady Bunch squares on screens & air kisses with our loves. We are tired of not being able to answer babes when they stop playing & run across the yard to ask *when will the virus be over?*

Aren't we tired? Sometimes too tired for the dishes & sometimes too tired to text back. It is 2020. We might run into each other masked in the market (the only risk we take these days) & even though we know we should not stand here & talk long it is *so*

good to see your eyes in real life. You'll say you're terrified
& I'll agree. It's all terrifying.

Here we are on the continuum of holding & being held in a line
where there is no semblance of fairness & still—no one ever
dreamed moments of our dystopian future would be so beautiful.
As in: a pastel sunset is furied across the early summer sky &
thousands of bodies in hundreds of streets sigh in exasperation
at the same time & dream together our spell could collapse an
unjust empire. We dig deeper into what hasn't been unearthed.
Maybe we want this to be *their* racism but when we look closer
we find it in *our* bodies. A muscle tightening on a sidewalk, a
vague epigenetic fear, an orphaned belief we forgot to pull at
the root. Theirs. Mine. Mine. Theirs. Ours.

How are our hearts? Our hearts no longer have savvy answers
or comfortable answers. This is how we hold each other.
Reminding ourselves as we emerge from dark rooms lit by
tiny screens: the sun still shines & the earth is warm under
our feet. No one is stopping us from walking over to the roses,
enjoying the wet grass, touching each new purple leaf, plucking
what is withered & sounding an instant prayer for new growth.

Nothing is predictable. Every option is on the table. Nothing is stopping us from looking for what is alive in this mess & saying hello.

We can feel our hearts here. It hurts. But we can feel our hearts.

We do not go back or forward to claim ourselves. We go in. The way in is smaller than we are & so we must squeeze through this impossible channel to arrive on the other side of the cosmic fabric & once we get there breathing can be excruciating & it is too bright sometimes & if we are even a smidge lucky someone somewhere will look at us like *we* are poetry.

How is my heart? Begging for life full-strength even if it makes my eyes water. Dear poet priestesses, bless you for taking our hands & leading us right to the edge, for asking why a heart only beats hard *right here*—& for making us want to stay. ♦

ASH GOOD
INITIATRIX, HIGH PRIESTESSES OF POETRY

poems in / THE WORLD

3	i don't know how to write a poem about systemic racism *Gabby Hancher*	
4	If all my failures were beads . . . *Ahuva S. Zaslavsky*	
5	Virus. Virus. I Love You. *Holaday Mason*	
10	The World Keeps Turning *Andra Vltavín*	
13	Revolution *Samantha Cimino*	
14	Unexpected Conversation at Mid-life *Dawn Thompson*	
16	With Liberty and Justice for All *Andra Vltavín*	
18	846 *Sierra Vida Lisa*	
20	us? beautiful / prepared for our own demise *Ash Good*	
23	The Gravitron *Beth Melnick*	
24	what frees *Sierra Vida Lisa*	
26	The Goose *Birch Dwyer*	

in / NATURE

29 At the Park
    Ahuva S. Zaslavsky

30 Forgiving Rain
    Beth Melnick

32 curious to know
    Lunita Valeria Velásquez

34 What Hums the Body Open
    Holaday Mason

38 Arrange Your Branches
    Samantha Cimino

39 our radical hands
    Ash Good

40 Rains return to Oregon as
    Ruth Bader Ginsburg transcends
    Jenn Lalime

43 Hands
    Samantha Cimino

44 you are preciousness
    Gabby Hancher

45 The Barren
    Beth Melnick

46 Burning
    Dawn Thompson

48 Pultrichude
    Holaday Mason

in / LOVE

51	the cypress knows our secrets	*Lunita Valeria Velásquez*
53	taut center / loose edges	*Ash Good*
54	Unexpected Conversation at Mid-life II	*Dawn Thompson*
56	Self Love Premonition	*Samantha Cimino*
58	Now, as it has always been	*Jenn Lalime*
59	The Spatial Province of an Oath	*Holaday Mason*
62	i want to kiss her in the morning	*Lunita Valeria Velásquez*
64	*but can novelty be our gender?*	*Ash Good*
66	what lingers	*Sierra Vida Lisa*
68	look at you baby self	*Ash Good*
69	we are not prey	*Gabby Hancher*

in / **PATTERN**

- 71   A Long Dead Horse
  Holaday Mason

- 73   The Fledgling
  Birch Dwyer

- 75   Sandwich
  Jenn Lalime

- 76   You tell me to be happy . . .
  Ahuva S. Zaslavsky

- 78   I'm a little girl asking Grandma why her pantry is full of canned goods. "For the End Times," she says.
  Dawn Thompson

- 80   i rode into the depths of grief on a sea dragon's back
  Gabby Hancher

- 82   Bifurcate
  Beth Melnick

- 84   Between Crevice and Stone
  Samantha Cimino

- 86   After Talking to Mom about White Privilege
  Andra Vltavín

- 87   Summer Gestures
  Ahuva S. Zaslavsky

- 90   Ouroboros in String
  Andra Vltavín

in / HOME

93   Things my daughter said to me before she went off to college (but then didn't go off to college)
Jenn Lalime

96   First Days of a Pandemic
Dawn Thompson

98   hummingbird songs
Sierra Vida Lisa

100   A Tree Never Eats Its Own Fruit
Andra Vltavín

102   Salvation
Jenn Lalime

104   Contentment
Dawn Thompson

106   After Joy Harjo: "For Calling the Spirit Back from Wandering Earth in Its Human Feet"
Lunita Valeria Velásquez

108   Calling Spirit Back
Samantha Cimino

110   The flushing mechanism is broken . . .
Ahuva S. Zaslavsky

in / BODY

113	What It Is to Eat *Birch Dwyer*	
115	spiral *Gabby Hancher*	
116	Hard Ones *Jenn Lalime*	
118	i haven't *Ash Good*	
120	To Fill The Void *Samantha Cimino*	
122	Out of the Blue *Dawn Thompson*	
125	let this love take any form it likes *Gabby Hancher*	
126	Basement Sink Communion *Birch Dwyer*	
128	intimacy waltz *Gabby Hancher*	
129	Spider *Holaday Mason*	
132	421 Million Yards *Andra Vltavín*	

in / DREAM

135	Cosmic Love	
	Samantha Cimino	
137	Living the Dream—2020	
	Jenn Lalime	
138	The Divine Whispered You Into Being	
	Beth Melnick	
139	From the Mountains to the Prairies to the Oceans White with Foam	
	Holaday Mason	
144	The Great Regression	
	Ahuva S. Zaslavsky	
146	Menopause	
	Birch Dwyer	
148	The Blue Dog	
	Holaday Mason	
151	how safety can feel like a frightened bird	
	Gabby Hancher	
152	Four Seasons of Hibernation	
	Andra Vltavín	
154	awake	
	Ash Good	
156	ACKNOWLEDGMENTS	
159	ABOUT THE POETS	

I'm a resonant body
  With knuckles and lungs
    Beat me with cymbals
      Play chords on my tongue

        I'm a resonant body
          With elbows and toes
            Drum on my rib cage
              Release my dissonant tones

— MAGGIE ROGERS

in the World

GABBY HANCHER

i don't know how to write a poem about systemic racism

i won't be able to do this the right way
want to unwind myself from the urgency i wear
like a militarized badge
i am prepared to make a thousand mistakes
interrupt the trauma loop i keep violently repeating
so that safety becomes a birthright to all bodies

not just white ones like mine

♦

AHUVA S. ZASLAVSKY

*

If all my failures were beads, they would make a nice long necklace.
And if ever invited to a party
again, I might wear it on my neck to complete my glorious look.
And at the party, my long necklace will get tangled in someone
    else's hair or jacket.
Maybe it will be you.
And you will look at me with great sorrow and hold my right arm
    and apologize
for breaking my necklace.
And I will tell you not to worry, and that it is all my fault.
I should not have worn such a long necklace to this crowded place.
And while we shout in each other's ears, very close,
    I will watch all the beads being beaten by dancing shoes,
    rolling from one stranger to another, looking for me.
And I will put my arms on yours and ask if you want to dance.

♦

Virus. Virus. I Love You.

What do they want, so many of them?

Murders of crows, then a video text

blurs the author faceless, oh yes,

my own boneless mirage the life behind

me a soiled wedding veil dragged

ragged but honest perhaps

& wearing my mien I choose to sing

really loudly, the town fool escaped

free wheeling while in every street

so many walk frightened, masked

souls clawing north where the mountains

melt again in a mist clamoring

with memory, history, so many bodies

up avenues starkly scared, no map

for these six-foot distances, we

can only wave across space hopeful

as messenger pigeons slipping

on a sea of ice—no chart for fear—

but a list of words might comfort

(don't overthink this)—alphabet,

salutation, sneeze, swerve, calculate,

turntable, pot-roast, intercourse,

inoculation, intercourse, sigh, sign—

I trust splendid beauty as I trust the way

a black cat does not remain whole

but disintegrates then reforms

as she veers between raindrops, elegant,

calm while, yes the homicidal reels

of crows unwind & offer their dark handshake

as if to say fare-thee-well, goodbye yesterday
(what had we imagined would happen?)

& I salute the naked daylight pouring down

around us—*plague* seems an antique word,

now a modern dance our babble heads

nodding polite to each other while thinking

of dying alone in some hospital's neon

triage, saying kiss me, cradle my death skull,

be the singer, the holy moment—as the body,

insistent on survival, breathes the eternally

mythic end, travels like a horn blown

hard, no warning, warring—a masked,

man runs the empty gray highway

screaming his head off inside

his own head but keeping it private—

his life a loaf of bread, a bar of soap, a bowl

of temperance, a broken thermometer,

the golden pear he's been given

so he can retrieve, revive, rewrite it

over & over desperate for perfect

symmetry, the spine of all lies, a fuck-all

warzone of bottomless will—my larynx

raw, mottled arms like doves fatigued

from holding up the cloche of my

small history, one like any other, motile

as weather, as stepping off a train that just

keeps moving forward & I have fallen

in love even inside the crash of the world,

fallen like a nude woman curling

up in new story—so easy to do really when

the book of the sky opens & drains,

covering everything completely

in tiny un-namable sapphire flowers.

♦

ANDRA VLTAVÍN

The World Keeps Turning

No one tells you
how to fill out demographic information
on your father's death certificate

after his sudden, unexplained death.
No one tells you the creditors
will start calling before the body's cold.

No one tells you of the need
to inform the woman your father
had an affair with

on an international number.
Leave a voicemail in Spanish: *Tengo información*
importante sobre mi padre, Domingo . . .

No one tells you how to decide
whether to pull the gold teeth out
of his skull.

But, most especially, no one talks
about the way grief really acts
in the body, how you wake up

the next morning after little or no
sleep, how none of your muscles move
because they know every part of you

has a piece of him.
And no one tells you, even though
your heart is shattered

like the water bottle you slam into the floor,
that your body will ache
in all the "wrong" places, guilt wrapping

itself around the void within you
as unwelcome arousal
demands—like the rest of the funeral arrangements—

to be tended. And you can ignore it,
wish it away, deny yourself, but
it will find you in your dreams. So,

if you are truly an activist in pleasure,
you will understand that this
is a part of grief because it must be.

This helps your father cross
to another side. This will unlatch
the gates that hold back tears.

Make a deal with the vibrator
you rarely remember to charge, offer
what small joy you find here to the spirits,

and release this blasphemy because
you are human, and the body
keeps moving just as the world keeps turning

after the pain and humiliation of death.

♦

SAMANTHA CIMINO

Revolution

Rest is revolution for traumatized bodies.
The body: such a sacred creation,
mangled into submission in infinite ways.

. . . Ride the waves. Sometimes you have
to hold your breath and submerge into
the vast mystery of ocean.

The ocean: our light bodies, singing
and screaming. Merging and transforming.

Transformation was never easy, but
it is inevitable. Change is the only
constant.

The world turned upside down. It will
take us all, but we can turn the wheel.

As it turns, veils get torn. How much
unveiling can we take?

I knew we'd be here. I will always
sing with you.

♦

DAWN THOMPSON

Unexpected Conversation at Mid-life

fast flurry full
go
make it happen
finish it up

and there I am
and there I'm not

Kneel,
says the Buddha,
who I've never spoken to in my life.

Bow,
he says,
and then continues on before I can interrupt him.

When I sit cross-legged, he chants, *the world stops spinning,*
slows
stills
sings.

Do you see the way the sun tosses his light to you, a rose for your hair?
he asks.
Do you hear the opera of rain outside your window?

Breathe
Breathe
Breathe,
he hums, looking very pleased with himself.

I have to admit
he has my attention.

Ah, he laughs, satisfied.
That's all I've ever wanted.

♦

ANDRA VLTAVÍN

With Liberty and Justice for All

I'm a libra, Mom says,
so I couldn't be racist if I tried,
and this is a worse bastardization
of astrology than newspaper horoscopes.
But, as my mother's daughter
and a libra rising, I ponder
what balance means when the fulcrum
is compromised, what *neutral* means
in an echo chamber.
I want to ask new questions—
who made these scales and why
must we measure in the first place.

Abolish the police. Abolish
the police. Abolish—
so this is the first time
someone in my family is an abolitionist
as I betray my maiden name—
my mother's maiden name,
my grandmother's maiden name—
in favor of a new legacy.

I am one person crying for the injustices
that never happened to me, one
person inside a self-organized organism
wheezing through a filtered mask to chant:
I can't breathe. I can't breathe.
I keep my body in shape for this
because when thousands march 52 blocks,
they don't stop for me.

If anything should die in our evolution,
it is this superiority complex.
None of us can be the hero; it takes hundreds,
thousands, hundreds of thousands
to shift power from masters
who tipped scales for 400 years.
So, no, Mom, your astrological alignment
will not protect you
when your definition of neutral
is to stand directly in the way.

♦

SIERRA VIDA LISA

846

heartbeat quickens
muscles stiffen
a cop murders in daylight
not rich, nor white,
under U.S. knife,
a false $20 warrants life

how many angles
witnessed to resound?
BLACK LIVES MATTER
as traumas compound,
seven generations lost,
imprisoned on no ground

incarceration nation
rings Wall Street's bell,
streams indoctrination,
profits from hate's spell,
death counts rising
as CEO pockets swell

behind picket fences,
beneath pages of history,
reform cannot transform
systemic white supremacy

from the land of the free,
this American Dream
is brought to you by slavery

♦

ASH GOOD

us? beautiful / prepared
for our own demise

Vanport, Ore., Sept. 26, 2020

for awhile we live that revolution
       follow both of them in riot gear
no stopping now i say
       it hits me before it hits me
    oh
how often do i hover just outside

radio   crackle   /   broadcasted   warning   /   proud   boys

on   the   move   /   tension   /   big   fields   /   stacked   cars

few   exits   /   locked   portajohns   /   dumpster   to   pee   behind

& this is all true

spies / no real names / police / affinity groups
tactics / probably guns / visible weapons are
a liability / black bodies / so much ballistic armor

maybe even the memory is dangerous—
this dream, that body
convinced of future we may never land in

little we each know to do our part / head-to-toe black
bloc but dope sneakers / calls for eye contact & trust
gravity / real-time / history / in ribcages / heartbeats

i know exactly what this city looks like
i can't shake that i really love you stranger—
have you ever felt more human?
more flawed & unstoppable?

there is a radiant black woman / live yellow bloom

in her bullet proof vest / when i ask you to imagine

a flower / the whole thing fits right there in your mind

open your eyes
hope you survive

◆

BETH MELNICK

The Gravitron

This kind of anger always pools in the belly
These tears are shame and grief
A laugh covers for me while
My fear pukes its heart out in a bathroom stall somewhere

I have to ask—where am I, in all of this?
This spinning that holds me at the edge of myself, paralyzed?
Am I not, also, the attendant at the center of this Gravitron?
Am I not the Gravitron?

Call Stop

◆

what frees

what frees us
from this system
that one kind defined
to name thieves winners,
blood trails behind?

what frees us
from our silos
so obsessed with *me*,
Capitalism's Cult,
to trust in *we?*

what frees us
from protection
against fear designed
to keep us busy,
blind to the dime?

what frees us
from checked boxes,
lies of normalcy,
to embrace unique
complexity?

what frees us
from chasing norms,
narrowly confined,
lives spent comparing,
lost in our mind?

what frees us
may be a breath,
sparking unity,
to question our trust
in falsity

♦

BIRCH DWYER

The Goose

At Regency Lake the freeway roars
beyond the chain link fence, wind whipping plastic bags
through its metal maze. *It's so peaceful here*,
Mom says. *I love the calm water.*

Styrofoam cups bobble in algae as wind
ruffles the wide lake. We tick our way forward
along the walkway, that cane Dad painted for her
marking our time. I answer her questions again

and again: *Where are you living now?*
Your husband does what for a living?
Even with dementia she is still the queen
demanding answers and I her subject, her cane

a scepter stamped into the sidewalk, my eyes
hard-set on water. Its ripples conspire
with light. Soon we will reach
that curve with the overflowing trash can

and the goose on her nest of sticks and plastic spoons.
She will look up at us as if we make one false move
she will lunge and bite, the long black curve
of her neck coiled against her white body.

I will make cooing noises at her as we pass,
offer thanks for her hard, dark eyes.
Mom will say again: *Oh the sweet mommy goose,
nestled with her babies*,

as she leans hard on my hand,
and I feel the length of my own dark neck
emerging from muscled shoulders.

◆

in Nature

AHUVA S. ZASLAVSKY

At the Park

She was watching the circle of barefooted women
turning around and around on the grass, their feet
wet from morning dew. Nothing magical or
mystical. In fact, pretty ordinary. Perhaps a new way
of practicing togetherness. Something she had heard of.
The grass is especially green today, she thought. It is
also quite ordinary, not to say earthy. A simple thinking
from bottom to top.
But then the sky turned milky-pink and almost touched
the grass. The circle was going too fast now, and the
grass was too slippery. How they can go on with no
sense of responsibility?
She couldn't pull herself up and made no voice while
the circle swiveled faster and faster, stirring in
ecstasy, mixing the pink sky and the wet grass together
into a Pink Lady cocktail, served by no other than
the great Dionysus.
She looks up and reaches her hands, willing to take
what is being served.

♦

BETH MELNICK

Forgiving Rain

Forgiving rain, dissolve me
My heart beats
outside its cage
Do hearts leave their nest?
Astral travel?
Are there two hearts?

Forgiving rain dissolve me
Dissolve my edges
Return me to myself
Become sand
Tree and sky
A song

Not a singular voice
but that of the river flowing
under this stage,
these curtains so fine, and light
Yet immovable
Except by magic

Forgiving rain dissolve me
So that i may pass and
join the stars
Become that
Symphony of ether

Forgiving rain dissolve me
So a child may draw me
from the ocean of consciousness
in a bright plastic bucket
and with me make a hole in the sand

Plump fingers, the tiny grains
creating irregular castle towers
Dissolve me
again and again
remembering and forgetting
everything and nothing.

♦

LUNITA VALERIA VELÁSQUEZ

curious to know

what drenches spaces
left vacant
words almost said
(not quite)
turn volume down
on newfound silence
or maybe
always there
nervous chatter
band aid fix
without the reach
hands hungry
basket lays
on its side
scattered contents
lost in
tall grass

cliff jumping
found favorable
in moments
where the sun
is hot, sexy
mystic waters
rinsing clean
tender bits
all spread out
on shadow rock
every cave
i swam to
was empty
neptune led
all the mermaids
home

♦

What Hums the Body Open

1

On a dark red rug, a young mother lies near the sleeping infant ivory hills of her hips twisted in a turquoise sarong rise & fall, the fractions of her maidenhood deconstructing, as she concentrates, allowing the feathers of the tree shadows that dust her arms to penetrate her animated, tender as she seeks the map of who she was, of how to continue anew.

2

A man, his head baldly touched by sun, stands in a field cloaked in pixilating clouds of butterflies painted ladies lifting & falling from the floral horizon at just the right time of year—carried windward over the Atlas peaks, some faded, dust laden, shred with years of flying, pastel failing stars craving the lush home of the sward, where the man prevails in love, sharp focused, mind emptied of all questions as he simply watches the turquoise, candle wax, lavender wings glowing in springtide, urgent to land & gently carpet the earth, he feels their rise & decent as they feed & fly, brushing too against his face, his whole body quivering & awake.

3

For a portrait, the woman nude, stands against a wall of dark foliage, slim hips of a boy one could love, her blue mask slipped halfway off halfway on, mouth open with inaudible words—a childlike flat land of satin breasts, how she wants to run the drought dusky hills barefooted, wild as coyote, chasing her own nocturnal forms into spring, her masks—the golden one near the lemon tree ripe with fury, the gruesome grand coal face hidden in wet crushed clover where she got scratched, where she screamed a landscape of light like bees face then tilted her open lips to the white poison blooms of the oleander. —

4

For no real reason the pen just breaks. Viscous black ink pools in
      my fingerprints

& I tattoo my torso, inking my breasts slowly in a chart of new
curiosity, twin trees of legs splayed opened on indigo bedding,
the damp triangle deep privacy slightly open again—The ink, the
silver silk of what is inner, until my hand simply rests on my ribs &
dreams construct the future of this body while I watch the trees
explode at the hearth of the full moon, leaves shivering & flying in
wide circles like pearled birds breaking hard through the stained
glass, the smudged redness of waking. Wake up says the bird at my
window. Some might say I was not careful enough

& I might reply some simply cannot feel real love.

♦

Arrange Your Branches

You can arrange your branches
  as lovingly as you would like.
You can drink in the sun, the light, the sky.
You can unfurl your roots
   into the damp earth
  pull it up through your bones.
You can let go and surrender,
   feel her holding you.
Let it open your eyes
   to a different frequency.
Let your heart beat
   to natural rhythms
Let the deep caverns become one with your being
  and the deep waters mix with your blood.
If you are still, you can feel this,
   the deepest of embraces.
If you are quiet, you can hear this,
   a song arriving on the wind.

♦

ASH GOOD

our radical hands

upturn deep-rooted garden
                    dig out denied metamorphosis
      what strangles
          fingernails flush with nature
                    compost history
          build altars to demolition
mix blooms & thistles
          bring wild inside
      pinecone rubble
        on our shrine
                    a vine's root nubs
          feel for earth
what do we reach for if
          we ask *do we want*
      anything we can remember?
        let us trust breath
                    returns after clearing
          fold ruins into more
tools for more hands
        it is time
     grab yours
        we will salve our blisters with what we plant

♦

JENN LALIME

Rains return to Oregon as Ruth Bader Ginsburg transcends

Sept. 18, 2020

Sea cave exploring
beneath blue sky
cloud breaks at Cape
Lookout our lungs
full of rain cleansed
air when we hear

I buckle there
at the mouth—black
stone cleaved by time
branchy barnacles
muscles iridescent
black blue purple green
sea anemones
bright and blurry

The tide hours out
reveals endless
intricacies—

a cathedral to
delicacy
resilience

Walking back to camp
you spy a sand
dollar—perfection—
which I pluck from wet
earth and pocket
you say it will
be okay and in
my desperation
I believe you

Free from forest
fires September smoke
we inhale deeply
like we haven't
in days—grateful

gullible—counting
on one woman to
hold back History
hold back hate

Back at camp my
pocket reveals
only sand and
bits of broken shell
gutted again
this time by hubris
having thought I
could carry such
fragile beauty
in my pocket

♦

SAMANTHA CIMINO

Hands

There is no escape from the crumbling
of the tower. We all choke on the
smoke of it. Some of us are more prepared,
aware of demons lurking.

Some still grasp at ignorance, blindness, a lie.
Refusing to hear the pleading scream of
life. We were meant to use our hands
to help. To prune the shrubs, to harvest, to
mend, to caress, to create, to feed ourselves.

Not to harm. We all have power within our
hands. I think of the warmth I feel in them,
sending out love. I think of fingernails
sturdy enough to pluck the new leaves
of an herb, rubbing between my fingers
and bringing them to my nose, the scent
a love poem to my body.

In society's rejection of nature, we have created
our own wilderness, seemingly more cruel
and chaotic. Again, trying to survive, grateful
to survive. There is no escaping the language
of nature.

you are preciousness

when skull echoes for days on end / when body constricts contracts concaves and calls it truth / when inner survivor slashes the throats of invisible foes satisfaction in each sound death / when eyes fresh from mornings' dizzied thoughts catch green and retouch abundance / when moan-wrapped bodies ache after separation from a momentary lifetime of union / when tender heart widens and the women of your lineage roar *speak* / when the word *no* slips sideways from quaking lips for the first time

then, too

◆

BETH MELNICK

The Barren

Angry for no clear reason, aware there is reason
just not in this body
or this mind
at this moment

Running in a desert of unwilling
uncooperative
underwhelmed
underwater

I remember that if I sit long enough, even in a dry lake bed
I will eventually see small animals and tiny plants
I will remember that nothing is truly
or totally barren
That even I am not barren

So here I sit in the grit
at the base of my bones
Waiting...

♦

Burning

It's the Autumn the world comes to an end.
The trees on fire,
the sun a small, red ember in the sky.
The fires move as fast as a panther over the parched ground
through small towns, farms, forests, fields.
Afterwards, where the panther has fed,
there is only carcass, ash and the foundations of home.

What lingers is the wretched witch of smoke.
The smoke travels hundreds of miles as if by magic,
laying her dark cloak over the people.
We cannot breathe, cry the people from behind their masks.
I cannot breathe, moans the earth.
We cannot breathe, croak the birds.
I cannot breathe, whispers the Black man as he is held down.

What lingers after fire is smoke.
What lingers after smoke is fear.
What lingers after fear is anger.
What lingers after anger is hate.
What lingers after hate is separation.
What lingers after separation is longing.
What lingers after longing is reaching out.
What lingers after reaching out is connection.
What lingers after connection is relationship.
What lingers after relationship is tolerance.
What lingers after tolerance is trust.
What lingers after trust is unity.
What lingers after unity is love.

♦

Pulchritude

—For Celeste Anne

Beautiful, she uses the word " pulchritude" & I can't recall what it means—me, a poet, near fifty nine, I have to ask & do as the man next door drags the garbage cans to the curb while the small town rises to Sunday, the fallen blooms of the late magnolias lining streets, filling now with September students bound for winter, yet clinging hard to summer—I watch them while she explains the word—the nature of arcane treasures—of cleavage, sparked allure, gold tan skin, or white, ebony, or brown—young women in tube tops & cutoffs, halters, bikinis, hip huggers sashaying PINK across the ass, flashing the final inch of butts & thighs, the rules of young muscles rippling fierce with aromas of dark musk, of diving in & drowning in the hidden temple, a rose tattoo at the gateway like a sentinel—pulchritude, comeliness, pulp & pulse, plunge of round, flood full, straining cloth tight over the unbreakable, pliant yielding smooth supple forbidden fortune cookies of sheen, lip gloss polish, lid glitter, moist skin on all sweaty curves, plump hallways of animal cohesion, succulent wellsprings molding the shapes of this world to gauze & silk, to elastic scarlet wobble of Spanx—mesh, mash, satin, rich form itching the hands of humans craving to stroke, hold, grasp, flow with the choirs of bottoms, breasts, tummies, the inescapable weather of nude shoulders, lustrous secrets, rippled, kneaded, molded—these bowls of bones pummeled into dreamscapes of a lasting flesh heaven, the clay of our bodies, the stuffed sheaths, dizzying enchantments of the long brown, black, red, blond hairs, the shaven, creamy sheerness, the tawny silk, loved, all globes of sugar, loved, tree sap, ore, unspoken guttural operatic howls, loved, annunciation, loved, corridors of desire, baskets & tables of flesh, of fem, of cock, loved, of babies & union—oh pulchritude, the last supper, the reason for black dresses & lacy undies, for prayers & food, sirens, siren, spiral of rapture, young bodies all over the place perfumed & everywhere promenading the main drag of Sunday before they fly away like seed pods.

♦

in Love

LUNITA VALERIA VELÁSQUEZ

the cypress knows our secrets

but i am relieved, been wanting to tell
that your kiss brings me
into the void soaked cerulean sweetness
i have only felt in dreams,
the kind of sleep that
makes the sheets hot
& morning return too soon

night walks sharing my coat pocket
queer cookie,
i became the big spoon
but i do not mind because
your hand on the back of my neck
melts me soft & fuzzy
i am that tiger year
you have not met yet

we go easy, tenderly
combined past experiences,
the ones where we failed
& where we almost won

somehow hearts forward still
streaming new, inhale

you meet me, i am knowing you
as i reach for the ladder
to climb a little higher
& string the moonstone
for when the darkness crawls in
a n d
i finally jump in to that
cerulean void soaked sweetness
that comes when my mouth says,
"alright let's try"
right into yours

♦

ASH GOOD

taut center / loose edges

pulled / in

                                      severed / stem

               gerbera /sips

caress / petal

                                              smooth / creased

       breathe / dissolve

                               young / ancient

                                              all i also am

    savor a guiltless tryst

                                        re: / fidelity—

      our cosmos never asked

♦

DAWN THOMPSON

Unexpected Conversation at Mid-life II

Let's make our stories love stories,
the blue, glass Buddha I bought the other day at the Goodwill said.

Why not? I replied,
though I knew my stories sometimes got away from me,
though I knew the anxious narrator loved to hear his own voice speak.

Let your stories lift you into a new version of yourself,
the Buddha suggested.
Okay, I answered,
though the plot sometimes got stuck on the same note,
though there were days my stories came out as
tragic tales that could make you weep.

Love it all while you can,
crooned the Buddha in my ear, then added,
You are the flame keeper.
You are the words searching for wings.

All I could do was nod.
I knew he was right,
for when I turned off the light,
I saw that blue glass friend
sitting on the table
glowing in the dark.

♦

Self Love Premonition

What's your name? She's here in front of me, I can feel her. Is it a mirror? We roll in ethereal light, we laugh and hold each other. How old are you? 33 we say at the same time. Is this a kind of love? Always looking for my twin.

Always looking for my sisters. I catch her in glimpses through wide brown eyes, through long black hair even if it is fake, through a shy smile, through whimsy and through laughs and through words and through facts.

In the mirror I see the depth of the river, the beauty of it, the movement of it, fleeting and uncapturable. A beauty that cannot be coveted. Is that what sex is? Coveting beauty? All the ways we cannot make love to the rivers, to the mirror, to the trees, the moon, the earth; and all the ways we can.

I love myself unconditionally like I love you. Meaning I know I have flaws, and I'm annoying sometimes, and I have stupid habits, but I'm also wow fucking amazing and brilliant and creative and deep and intelligent and that kind of outweighs it all. Do you know what true power is? It's love.

Like the witch in her cottage who crafts all kinds of things with her powers, a whirling mess, yet some kind of chaotic order. Things spiraling in the air. That is how I create. Maybe nobody sees from outside the cottage what is really in there, maybe now and then they see the glow radiating from it, or they hear some strange sound, or distant singing, maybe the weeds grow wild and the ivy covers the house and the flowers get taller and bigger and the branches seem to embrace it, maybe they wonder but maybe not. If someone were to open the door I wonder what would happen.

She opens the door, and a huge wave swallows her up.

Last night the moon was full, and I couldn't even look at you. I was somewhere else. And you talked about meaningless things, and I barely replied, and you barely noticed. And I knew that you didn't really know me at all.

♦

JENN LALIME

Now, as it has always been

The genesis
of heartbreak—
remember—is an
inestimable love

The body itself
a slingshot cradle
stretched taut
to free longing

We endure only
in our suppleness
and what we chance
in ammunition

The heart itself
a quiver cradling
infinity—unknowable
and not even ours

It's just I wish
for you to wake
each day a poem
on your tongue

♦

HOLADAY MASON

The Spatial Province of an Oath

1

I still owe you a birthday gift—that one un-filled small promise to

brush your white hair, peel a ripe pomegranate—engrave

a crescent moon

in the molted reddened chain-mail of its rind, break it open with my

teeth before we wash our shoulders & faces in its tender bleeding.

So many conversations these days are of what we cannot have.

Yes & of course of what we do—

how the bed sheets smell of milled slumber, surrendered remembrances

of our own skin & sweat blended with the others, the one's

who keep us in time.

How, like worn rags once used for polishing antiquated silver we will

ring this terrible year out until we shine—our bodies ornaments,

gleaming celebratory fruits—we, all of us—

I still owe you that old birthday gift, to realize what's unfulfilled—

my vow to brush your winter hair, test its unexpected weight,

those drifts like hearty wild grasses we can build houses of,

substantially thick spilling over my slight uneven hands until the

rhythm of what is braided—one, two, three, repeatedly grows,

circles, merging together, the past, the present, the future—

that heavy luxurious fabric.

2

Vow

 I still owe you

A small promise Unfulfilled

Your white hair

A ripe pomegranate Marked A crescent of crooked teeth

Breaks/broken open Flows Slightly uneven

Tenderly Bleeding

Polishing us Like ornaments

Curious gleaming Fruit

Our bodies

♦

LUNITA VALERIA VELÁSQUEZ

i want to kiss her in the morning

sheets and faces, slightly crumpled
coffee brews in the background,
aromatic signature of simple good
body so expanded it becomes water
allowing heart awareness to hold
lover's river without allowing leaks
to fall through fingers or words
that needed to be said for safety

maybe we shower, sharing my space
creating room because when i hide
i hurt me more, a butterfly wing
creased by the closing window
why would i ever? instead open
full flight, and leftover soup
for tomorrow we lunch in the sun
and i know her more, this creature
who chose me to love

tender bits stinging at the reminder
that the right loving is steady, patient
tender bits sting because this all new

gentle repair for the ways it was taught
in a different way, many times over
sweetie brown eyes just gaze
no rushing there, come whole
becoming fruit in warm embrace
soft touch, i melt, purring
well fed tiger silent feet

pour the coffee, frothy milk
this poem arrives and i know
this might meet her there
a howl sent through silence
stirring, no tether found
liberation not had before
in another time when we
tried this and
now i kiss her in the morning
no hiding, no secret
paint a mural of it
finally time said yes

♦

ASH GOOD

but can novelty be our gender?

i text mid-night   you reply   *!!!!!!!!!!! ha if it can be that's what*

i am   in daylight our soft anatomy is unambiguous   at collins beach

for respite from revolution   questioning   when is right to rest? what

is right to do?   pulled between neck-high submersions in fast-moving river

& crawling back goosebumps to sun   my body bare & warming   your skin

dancing in ink that won't wash   charcoal fingerpainted from found firelog

leaf-filtered light exactly how i like

                                          imperfection abounds but here you are

a renewed sliver of sublime creature to soak in   novel   ballcap half-hiding

my gaze   child chases father   splashing water   bottoms less bronze than

tangle of limbs   my ankle still tender from nonlethal munition   i can't forget outside forces intend to separate   skin from element   skin from

skin   sand   water   curious fly   body   creation   origin

perfection   what isn't

                                          we can't ignore when wind picks up or what lies

ahead   i'm collarbone deep in the unknown again   you offer myths

our past selves wrote to tend our future   i don't know where i came from

but i do know   during this very long week   naked by the columbia

is the closest i'm getting back to it   when we first get here you say

we've come so far   this might as well be another realm

& it is

♦

what lingers

what lingers is silent
something close to dread
all that's left to accomplish
all that's yet to be said

what lingers is fearful
never enough time,
thoughts chatter, disorganized,
grooved anxieties chime

what lingers is wisdom
from life misaligned,
the cost to get lost in roles
i let others assign

what lingers is knowing
i can own what's mine,
boundaries can be magic,
practice builds a strong spine

what lingers is thankful
for all the before,
the lessons in discernment,
every knock at my door

what lingers is support,
chosen family,
a love without performance,
true reciprocity

♦

look at you baby self

in the mirror / bathroom by the gym / closest to darkroom closest to the theatre / quickest from freshman locker still ugly brown tile / new sink / fresh paint same drab door swings light / backpack heavy / shoulder tuck slump into resistance / before life pushes open / too-big cracks in privacy panels / always straight to largest not wanting closed in / caged regardless / endless hallway / baby angst / dragging feet / no way to know ourself yet / hard way our mind hits mirror every damn exit / oh baby self let's just take a / sweet jesus / hide in a stall minute here / today / look in an old mirror / i see you

♦

we are not prey

the heart hardens, stony & barren
on the backs of all who labor without dreams
must be shook from the inside out
until the guts are exposed
until the anger is rinsed clean from our systems
through hymns we've routinely been conditioned to forget
& when the grief finally claws it ways to the throat
it wails, inconsolable
let it be a love song for all who work to live
serenade the ones who forgot
we are made of animal bones
all snot & tears & blood
shaking like elephants—infinite wrinkles & wisdom
we were made for this moment,
to remember the bounty of our wide meadow hearts

♦

in Pattern

A Long Dead Horse

My thighs were split apple wine.
Under night skirts of cotton
you rode
white horses, broke sweat,
fell out of the cabin doorway
naked, for air,
dragging your mother's quilt
into the dust long before the
sun broke Crooks Mountain.

In between the stars,
across big sliced plateaus I watched
the headlights of a car lash zigzags
down the foothills towards Fresno
from far above the flat blade
of San Joaquin river

you had no chest hair at all.
Let me bleed all over the bedclothes,
then laughed beer stains and big thumbs
into my vagina, bruised my arms,
smelled the ink of my new tattoo
still burning with chlorine.

My ribcage shook
under your hands.
A wild peacock you crowed
before you licked me clean.

In the morning the whole river
smelled of fire. I studied how small lichen
was still clinging
to the cold sides of tree trunks
even after daybreak was everywhere
and the fingerprints of white spring grass
were shaken and blown away
into a growing rigid heat.

♦

BIRCH DWYER

The Fledgling

Today on the phone with your mother, you
on your kitchen stool and she
in bed at a care facility, she demands

a report from your day, a pleasant packaging
of news from the front. Though her body is under siege,
though she can't remember

the name of your son, she is still
the queen demanding achievement for the crown.
Her voice towers from a throne of crumpled sheets.

So tell me, what did my amazing and talented daughter do today?

This is no time to let a mother down, yet
you explain, with no embellishment
that you fiddled with a few poems, did your hip exercises

and walked the dogs through a field of mud.
Your truth-telling hangs in the air
like a note off-key.

That's it, Mom. That's all I got.

Her tumbler of tea stamps the bedtable
with an audible thump, a scepter for news that does not please.
I wish we could just have a conversation, you say.

The comment lands on the bare floor
of the hospital room like a young hawk
trying to gain its footing against slick tile.

♦

JENN LALIME

Sandwich

My mother
a child
my father
and I cared
for and when
she died
it broke us.

I tried a while
turned my eye
on him, but he
would not have it;
the caring.

So again—my
own children
grown (or at least
able to make
a grilled cheese
without me
hovering).

AHUVA S. ZASLAVSKY

*

You tell me to be happy
to take things
easy   to think
positive and even to forcefully
smile because it will increase my dopamine level
I smile and sigh   *I will try*
I say

I am built differently
I think
In the bathroom I stand
I look at me
Everything is pulling down   dripping
I feel like a plastic bag fished out of water
But I practice smile after smile after more
smiles   an addict on a street corner
begging her dealer to pass some of this dopamine
through the car window
in exchange for "how many smiles do you want to see"

Like the village fool
Like a circus clown
Like a character in the *La commedia dell'arte*

You are such a pleaser
Just an entertainer
Too attached to this mask   to this role
to the make-pretend

But it is me you are looking at   I see myself telling me
It is really you   *Ha, it is really me!*

Like theater curtains at the end of the play
I let my towel drop and I bow

◆

DAWN THOMPSON

I'm a little girl asking Grandma why her pantry is full of canned goods. "For the End Times," she says.

The people are staying home.
The people are taking to the streets.
The people are talking to their neighbors.
The people are dying.
The people are teaching their children.
The people are writing poems on the sidewalk.
The people are not shopping
not driving
not building
not traveling.
The people are sewing masks.
The people are praying.
The people are on fire.
The flames are quick and quirky.
The flames are the color of roses.
It is rose season.

The roses are resplendent,
scarlet, sunshine yellow, angel cream.
The people gather the roses.
The people bring the roses inside their houses.
The people shut their front doors.
Outside the front doors flames of protest
spread down empty, rose-lined streets.
Underneath the streets the earth is burning.

♦

GABBY HANCHER

i rode into the depths of grief on a sea dragon's back

terrified of drowning
labyrinth of loss & longing
ensnares our ankles

bodies of kelp could devour us whole
disappearing would be so easy
in this wide ocean

then feel the dragon's body
roll out onto rocky shore
among shells & detritus

scales crusted with barnacles
gasping salty sea air
amidst ghostly coastal fog

time travel on this
vast expanse of beach
between then & now

far enough still to watch waves
soften into memories
to forgive our amphibious selves

we seek solace under a tree
which has made its home here
shaped by wind & life, growing

sideways on a precipice as if to say
yes, i too am touched by change
and still i grow

♦

BETH MELNICK

Bifurcate

We leapt as the train bore down on us.
Slipped through a slit in the veil,
split apart.

My innocence jumped before I did,
before I understood what was happening, to me
in the dark.

Why does that big man throw baby bunnies
From the bridge . . .

Living bunnies? Yes.
It's what they did to his bunnies
So long ago

This is not a metaphor

They took his bunnies
slaughtered them in front of him.
Boy was 3 and 5 and 8
He split . . . apart

How gently the man-boy hands
release his shame, his pain, his love
To the road below
Watching the only things he loves
Taken away again and again

In the underpass
I squat next to a broken tent
wait, in a pink tank top.

Do not corner me
The best part of me flew long ago and . . .
left a beast with sharp teeth, strong reactions,
and a terrible need.

Below the overpass
Waiting, for innocence to return
I watch for the Easter Bunny.

♦

SAMANTHA CIMINO

Between Crevice and Stone

I am looking for the spaces in between
I am looking for the many faces
of self
Stalking the shadows into the caverns
and caves
amidst a violent ocean
A force so beautiful it makes the
knees weak
I want to ride the tide
smash into the rocks.
But my desires fall away
If I cannot taste the salty air
I must conjure the waves in me

I was so intent on breaking
this spell of isolation long ago
I was so intent on looking up
from shadows, finally
to shine

But no. So I am resigned to continue
this way I know so well,
and will know in a deeper way
To look at it from different angles,
to know all are here and there too

Isolation is an illusion

♦

ANDRA VLTAVÍN

After Talking to Mom about White Privilege

—After Gabby Hancher

I'm about to make a thousand mistakes,
but I pick up rainbow gradient yarn
every pattern told me not to use,
and crochet the single stitch mom taught
me as a child, now with less clumsy
fingers. I ask her the name
of the stitch I know, and she says
I can't possibly remember,
but I send her pictures of my progress
even while she is still angry.
So, I watch dozens of videos to learn
how everything works in spiral
and show her the result: a disc of yarn
to hold up when the conversation
becomes too heated. She says,
*I didn't think it would be so
complicated*, and I remind her
it only feels that way
in the beginning.

♦

AHUVA S. ZASLAVSKY

Summer Gestures

She sat in the familiar back seat of the old bright orange Volkswagen van. A large adventure book laid wide open on her bare thighs, like an atlas. The window was rolled down and a warm blanket of burning sun covered a stripe of her skin.

What quickens?

The car engine made a loud rattle. Dry, grainy road swung her legs, rubbing them on the 300-grit sandpaper fabric of the front seat's back. The front of the van was foggy. She could barely see the top of the two old heads swinging side to side, covered with heavy gray smoke.

What quickens?

Her stringy right arm reached out with open palm and stretched fingers. She let the summer wind push it back and forth—a broken vane in search of direction.

What quickens?

Now she opened and closed the space between her bony fingers, and the bright white light came through like lighthouse flashes. She was saving the flies and mosquitos from a tragic death on the windshield.

What quickens?

And she was not only saving the bugs from their fate but also keeping the words from flying off the page and out of her pockets through the window.

What quickens?

Her head rested on the headrest. Her dark long hair romped like an angry willow. The blue sky colored the darkness in her eyes.

What quickens?

Her hungry mouth was wide open, hoping to swallow each dusty cypress they passed. She greeted every crow that sat on the electric poles with a bow, and they greeted her back in awe.

What quickens?

And many roads will open and close.
And many paths will curve and straighten.
And the ochre fields will expand and contract.
And the heat will hug and release.
And the car will roam.
And time will take her home.

◆

ANDRA VLTAVÍN

Ouroboros in String

Learn an entirely new language

of stitches—circle,
box, puff, crocodile, and get grabbed

by the hook deeper into what is

more lifestyle than hobby—fiber,
mohair, merino, angora. And from there,

a short journey toward maiden and treadle,

toward orifice and leader. The leader
you choose for your first thread

is a scrap from a scarf you made

your grandfather. But still, there are more
words to this language, these mathematics

and space-filling curves—hand card,

hank, roving, draft. Your hands ache
from five hours of feeding fibers to themselves—

pinch, pull, keep tension, balance. How many

parts of your body can you involve?
Wash it, beat it, dry it, shock it, dye it, tie it,

all of it reminding you

you need yarn to make more yarn.

♦

in Home

JENN LALIME

Things my daughter said to me before she went off to college (but then didn't go off to college)

August 2020

What's for dinner?
Can I buy a skateboard?
Why are you looking at me that way?

I love you
I hate you
You've traumatized me for life

You're not listening to me
Don't touch me
Scratch my back

You already told me that (eye roll)
Stop making that noise with your mouth
Can I have the car keys?

I can't hear you (points to earbuds)
I can hear you—I just don't feel like responding
That's stupid

I want to kill myself
If you hospitalize me, I will never ever speak to you again
Ever

That's not what I said
That's not what *you* said
Oh my god, *yes*, I know

I love this
I hate this
I don't care

I'm hungry
Not for that
Never mind

Stop, you got almond goo on my phone
Can you rub my hands?
I don't want to exist anymore

I'm fine
Whatever
It's *fine*

Listen to this
Watch this
Read this

You *never* listen
Leave me alone
God!!!

♦

DAWN THOMPSON

First Days of a Pandemic

You drive the long 5 hours to get there
even though you can only stay less than 2 days
because at home there is a sweet boy with needs like high water after
    the rains
because the world is falling off its axis
because there is no toilet paper in the stores
and the words *quarantine, unprecedented, social distance*
are the mysterious call of a flock you've never seen

When you get to the house you grew up in,
your mom and aunt have been waiting awhile
you all sit together in the backyard under the cold sun
drink ice water
admire your aunt's pink, sparkly nails
note how much your mom looks like grandma now

You do ordinary things
rent a movie in the evening
go to the store the next day to buy cat food, a thermometer, a game
    to bring back to your boy
You don't hug your mom
You both wash your hands

look at the incisions from her surgery the week before
look up the latest news about the virus on your phones
your mom says she wishes your aunt would be more careful

The morning you leave for home you show your mom
a video clip of quarantined Italians singing their hearts out on their
    balconies
your mom, who is soft-hearted, starts to cry
You fantasize about having no family to return to
about moving upstairs
where you can be there for your mom if she needs you in the middle
    of the night

At the front door you finally hug your mom
She hugs you back, the risk of it like blood, like history
You realize you don't know when you'll see her again
Later you'll call, almost home, from a rest stop
where everything looks so normal you almost forget to ask
    how she feels

◆

SIERRA VIDA LISA

hummingbird songs

as i clear out my past
i make room for my future
snip all those stitches
softly pull on sutures

spring's light has me lifted
new patterns are gifted
paving fresh space
let my mind race

i sit,
come back,
and sit again.

i rest.

breath for creativity
space where i can truly be
looking back at evolutions
making way for new solutions

before rushing to
do or solve or make
it's the rest to digest
we underestimate

♦

ANDRA VLTAVÍN

A Tree Never Eats Its Own Fruit

—*After Ash Good & Dawn Thompson*

I'm collarbone-deep in
the unknown as I hold
this fruiting belly open—
I am ripe with want and ache
for satisfaction underneath
what will soon be a new moon,
and the world holds its breath
with me. I hear whispers

of future; I hear the match
Apollo will throw
from the sky but have no idea
where it will land, only
that it will burn, *quick*
and quirky with its flames—
I am ripe with possibility
like the cherries hanging

purple and know fruit
does most its rotting on the tree.
I learn to tell from the outside
which dark spots mean worms

even before my fingers press
into bloody flesh. I take what
this tree has to give and mash
everything to pulp, pink

with butter and honey. Five jars
of jam after the hours I labor—
I am ripe, will soon be overripe
with possibility and ache to collapse
down to only one pit, one seed
to save for the distant winter,
quick to give away
this unsweetened flesh. Please,

taste this experiment, let
the chill of preserved fruit pull us
one day closer to our own satisfaction—
the sugar of our tongues
sweetness enough.

♦

JENN LALIME

Salvation

—After Andra Vltavín

In my house there was always enough
clean towels, hot food, wine to drink.
I loved one man fiercely for over 30 years
raised two kids full force against their will
but did I improve the world? Who can say?

I have failed a fair number of times.
Proselytized and denied in equal measure.
Earned some money, breathed a handful
of poems out among the stars.
I've done a fine number of things
but did I touch greatness?

Not an expert in my field
no golden medals ring my neck
I never even got right with the Lord.
Did legacy call while I was washing
the dishes? Did I throw seeds
on fertile ground and forget
to watch them grow?

I loved and longed for what
I did not have. Took for granted
what I did, suffered right
alongside my fellow creatures
in this shared dream.
The magic is ready for you
was I not ready for it?

How to take stock?
Account for a life lived?
Not despair as we whisper
walk into this next
handful of uncertain years.
Learn the hard way we were
never playing for keeps.

♦

Contentment

turn away from the news
walk outside
where the moon hangs vigil
where stars pray

re-enter the bright orange door of your home
kiss your husband
who is watching the news
kiss him again
where his hair is turning gray

do not want anything in return

walk with soft eyes
from the living room to the small kitchen
remember all the days living in the walls
open the right kitchen cupboard above the stove
see a flowered field of post-it notes there
on the inside cupboard door

I love you
Have a beautiful day

look out the kitchen window
at the hummingbird feeder hanging in the black night
at the pear tree's silhouette
at the child's wet, green slide

know you are in the right place

walk back past your husband and the news
past the family photos on the hallway wall
to your son's closed bedroom door

stop

remember all the hard hours
when he was a pen stroke on a long list
of girls' and boys' names
you kept in your back pocket

open the door quietly and listen
for the soft wind of his breathing
make your way to him in the dark

♦

LUNITA VALERIA VELÁSQUEZ

After Joy Harjo: "For Calling the Spirit Back from Wandering the Earth in Its Human Feet"

and then what?
do i get to keep myself here
in the space where it feels good
and right
to inahle deeply
to feel my truth
when my spine curves
toward the sun and
back of the heart lights
in the knowing
that every piece that traveled
went well and far
only to find itself
never actually apart
from the silver black cords
of *abuela*'s braid

she holds proudly in
one strong fist
as we all dangle off of it
the place that kept us whole
as we bravely journeyed
life path comprised of
individual strands
of hair

♦

SAMANTHA CIMINO

Calling Spirit Back

—After Joy Harjo & Lunita Valeria Velásquez

Another day becomes night.
Oscillating between valor and terror.
Seeing myself in others,
　becoming a mirage as I expand
　　my awareness.
Coming back to myself.
My body. Aligned. Breathe.

Art film reminds me to slow down,
　it allows my fragments to settle and fuse,
　integrated again.

Prayer can feel like action,
　whispering to the flame.
Hope can feel like a burden,
　an overripe fruit.

Ideal for wine,
  ideal for pleasure,
    that is what we must remember.

The joy is down here, a mellow creek,
  that flows and cleanses and renews.

◆

AHUVA S. ZASLAVSKY

*

1

The flushing mechanism is broken so the water in the tank will flow nonstop. I don't flush. It is so quiet but now I can't stop hearing the toilet water running in my head.

Your thoughts have sounds.

2

Once I shared a room with a snoring friend. I used earplugs to sleep—very effective—no sound came through. Then something scary happened. In the complete silence of the night, friend deep asleep beside me, I suddenly heard two voices conversing in my head. I immediately removed the earplugs to listen—even though I knew it came from inside. It felt so real. Maybe my friend was talking or maybe I heard a couple arguing or fucking next door—the kinds of things that happen in cheap motel rooms when the separating walls are rice paper. Only, outside me it was deadly silent. I heard my heartbeat racing.

Close your eyes now.

3

My space heater rumbles—almost a seashell attached to the ear. Kids believe in this stuff—that the whole ocean is trapped in a shell. I don't need one to listen to the ocean. I have a space heater. Maybe a promise of ocean is for kids who can't go there—once I knew a girl who believed the ocean was right behind the mall in her desert town. I never took her there because I couldn't face the disappointment on her face.

Pause.

4

Sounds float out of my own shell. I hear things but I'm not crazy. We want proof that an ocean lives in a seashell or behind a desert mall.

Make a story.

♦

in Body

BIRCH DWYER

What It Is to Eat

My mother taught me that half-gallons
of ice cream were meant to be hollowed
out in one sitting, cantaloupe too, our spoons
a knife

against the rind, and that the raisins
in English muffins could be picked out one
by one, the fatty flour remains thrown
down the drain.

Now with a carton
of blueberries before me, I take you
one by one, hold each globe between my fingers
until I feel my own belly's rise and fall, imagine
the plant from which you came hugging

the ground with leaves like
spears, purple and pregnant
against pine-needled soil.
Blueberry, I roll you

against my fingertips
until your purple stain
claims me, place you
upon my tongue, tart

to mild,
firm to soft,
our stories dissolving
into my tongue.

♦

spiral

—After Joy Harjo, Lunita Valeria Velásquez & Ash Good

uncover humanity from beneath
a rock in grandpa's garden

dance with the worms & roly-polies
nature in process; pure delight

then wander the earth on human feet
which ache in all the wrong places

oh how this small wild sound looks
for a mouth to pour into

beauty was worms all along

♦

JENN LALIME

Hard Ones

Now that it's back
we'll talk about the Cancer
Did you feel that?
Did your belly drop?
If it did, fellow
traveler, read on.

You know the dread
waiting for lab results
conjured by the doctor's
name flashing across
your phone screen.

How quickly mortality
stirs at a cellular level
sits you right back down
in the dark place—

>   hospital waiting room
>   the surgeon's scalpel
>   up against my son's

>   carotid artery
>   recovery room where
>   he wept, begged me
>   not to leave his side—

That's mine
What's yours?

Those who've not
yet met this beast
ask easy questions:
Will he survive? and
When will it be over?
We hope and never.

Much harder to say
how we'll stare it down
each day hold on
to one another and heal.

◆

ASH GOOD

i haven't

1

since the artichoke bloomed / since i was shocked out of my foot bones / since it rained / since sun streamed through the prisms again / since yesterday's nap with the maple / since trumpet guy played in my driveway & a girl's shoulder oozed from non-lethal munitions & i gave away every cold la croix in the fridge to protester cheers *viva la revolucíon* / not since the ash starting falling again since the wind growled over the dinnerplate dahlia / since i accidentally sprayed myself full-tilt with the hose / i haven't since the fire caught / not since that first hug in months

2

when it's been this long & a dam breaks / do you too wonder is this pain or pleasure? / if i were trying to make a friend feel better i would say *you are good despite this gnawing pressure to be supernatural* / here have a recipe to laugh or cry or feel or write / get semi-alone & settle in the dark / exalted & also kneeling to yourself usually it is enough to say one basic truth out loud / *i am a person sitting on a floor / in a body i work so hard to know / in a space i have curated to call home*

♦

SAMANTHA CIMINO

To Fill The Void

Something heart wrenchingly beautiful
about the passion of voice
singing all the pain away.
To gather joy instead of sorrow,
to brew them together.
How our lungs can release emotion
like they release toxins.
Singing is the voice of the heart.

When I was so sad the other night,
I released my voice
singing into the void
singing to fill the void
singing until I am sobbing
feeling broken but alive.

I went for a walk; it was late
but I needed the air, the plants—
they are always here.
And again, the magical kitty
ran up to me delightfully;
my sorrows dissipated into the black sky.

Relations come in many forms,
but our rigid edges make us blind.
All beings speak, all beings sing
in their own way,
and we all want to share our hearts,
Listen, listen, listen.

♦

DAWN THOMPSON

Out of the Blue

She zipped up
buttoned up
polished her shoes
rolled up her sleeves
tightened her belt

pressed the wrinkles of her jeans
     with the palms of her hands

but underneath her collar
a storm was brewing

She could feel the winds
of herself
picking up though
it was a fine
     fine day

She could hear a drum
beating
inside her chest

a heart
drumming
THUNDER
drumming

then out of nowhere
smack
where they say the 3rd eye is
LIGHTNING

she tried to catch it
with her straw hat
but it shot a hole
      clean through

her hat off
her top button undone
her zipper broken
her shoes covered with muck

suddenly the wind was kicking up
a new dress around her
      red, gold and orange
she liked the fit

the sky splitting open
the rain
      unleashed
and she
undone

♦

GABBY HANCHER

let this love take any form it likes
—After Ahuva S. Zaslavsky & Ash Good

in my mind i unfold her like an atlas
bodies so expanded they become water
sugar that dissipates on the tongue
now invisible to the naked eye
but i taste it in my dreams
an exothermic reaction
to guide me home

◆

BIRCH DWYER

Basement Sink Communion

—For Meadow Road on the Sandy River Delta

Admit it—the reason you take
your white dog in the rain to that huge field
pebbled with puddles is not because

you relish the role of trudger, all-season hiker
or even martyr to family need, but because
you need to see his underside

flocked, like a chocolate-dipped biscotti
charging across a chain of lakes, because his bottom half
turns you giddy as your legs arc

across raindropped water
taking sky and storm cloud
two by two—

because you drive home
in a car smelling of pond scum, carry
his speckle-bellied body

down creaky stairs; because you heft him
into a worksink, slosh tumblers of warm water up under
a belly and over mermaidy tresses; because

your back aches; because the clothes dryer
tumbles, the coconut dog shampoo bubbles and your fingers
lather up hairy waves—

because this is your communion
with mess and fluff, your clearing of crusted hair,
your week's worth of snags

pulled clean; because as you towel
him off in the pricy bath sheet, slow down
your strokes to tired dog speed, he sneaks

a glance up at you
through the towely tumble,
this dog that cannot tolerate eye to eye
places one warm paw

on the top of your hand, his pause button
on this moment, his way of saying
Glad to be here. Slow down more.

♦

intimacy waltz

—After Beth Melnik & Ahuva S. Zaslavsky

my innocence jumped before i did
this time in the passenger seat
practicing grown up words
that roll around my pink tongue
      this conversation will swallow me whole
but the truth is, it felt good
to be needed like that
so i practice smiling neat little mouth lines
tracing myself limb from limb
so my head doesn't float away
from my baby body
as we ride together in the car

♦

HOLADAY MASON

Spider

Just waking, I watch,

as through mid air,

a being, its body

a small perfect pearl

spins from one plane

to another—

from soil in fact,

towards somewhere beyond

all I can see:

a doorway of sunlight,

rain gutter, roof eve,

the Jacaranda limb,

new pods & leaves,

a cloud washed sky

into which she weaves,

traversing a ladder

as sheer as wind,

through fields of air

on one simple thread

too light to bear,

yet tough enough

to carry her well

from one side

of the world

to the other.

♦

ANDRA VLTAVÍN

421 Million Yards

If ever I write an autobiography,
let it be made of string—
upcycled, repurposed, free, clearance,
wildflower landscape gradient, homespun Angora—
but then the string will need to be threaded,
woven, crocheted, knitted
just like rocket wires before a journey
to the moon—space travel
is always in my future. Cosmic stitches
will need new names, not single crochet, half-
double crochet, double crochet,
but quarter note, half note, whole note,
treble cleft—a musical naming convention
appropriated for measuring length not of sound
but of loops. And now that the most beautiful scarf
I have ever seen requires both
crochet and knitting needles, this is the moment
when my British fiber crafts walk
across my fingertips to Poland, to the Czech,
to Russia and knitting patterns
that never knew the simplicity

of a miniature shepard's hook.
This is how I rewrite history—
with thread and yarn and string
across a tangled ancestry
that has little to do with me
until I fashion it from nothing
and next-to-nothing. One dimension
becomes two, which becomes three
if I add sleeves, and there
we all are, in a garment fit for travelling
well beyond the stars.

◆

in Dream

Cosmic Love

to escape this tangled web
    we run
        we are thrust backwards
we light our hearts on fire
    a blazing love
a burning ache
    that pit of sorrow
        like volcanic mud
we sleep
    we awaken
        we dream
new worlds growing in our bellies
    seeds bursting
        with radiant hues
more colors than we could see before
    and the calls get louder
        echoing in our spirits
and we become holy
    beaming and bright
we are ecstasy

fusing together
a divine cosmic web
   powerful and alive
composting evil
   for fertile soil

♦

JENN LALIME

Living the Dream — 2020

the one with rooms under the house—
the moment you find yourself too many
floors down—no door in sight—you can't
remember what you need to remember

but now you're running through the airport
to catch that flight to walrus-knows-where
too many bags—bricks—at the
end of your arms realizing you left

the oven on before noticing no one
is in the driver's seat your belly sinks
your limbs don't move it's only
your mind clawing your way to the wheel

to take the test you forgot about until
you settle into that middle-row seat-desk
fluorescent lights the taste of chalk
and you are naked but for a mask

♦

BETH MELNICK

The Divine Whispered You Into Being

You are not putty
You are light
Listen to yourself as you float in a sea this . . .
The only true reality

When you look out
There you are, a speck of bright divinity
In every eye, in every word
in the movements of the ether

You are the atom
The explosion
You are sound
          . . .   and silence

You, are all that
Keep going . . .

You were made for this

◆

HOLADAY MASON

From the Mountains to the Prairies to the Oceans White with Foam

— Irving Berlin, 1918

My mother comes out of the darkness.

The tunnel is red, is opening, closing

like a wild poppy tracking day into night.

Under the floating indigo mountains,

there are no words, just this act as she pulses out

with her mother's black & white checkered apron

tied around her, sagging slightly as if the pockets

are full of peanuts or keys & she intends something.

I know this since her lips are moving—not unlike

a silent player piano in an empty formal dining room,

the table set with tarnished silver, no, there's no

discernable sound, only a slight humming

from the diagrams of history's shadows—

too many to count flinging from her chest

as she steps onto the black highway.

You check your watch to see where you are standing.

The sound is everywhere without sound, like a lie

you can glimpse, like a city of ether yet built of solids,

of minerals, of soils. We are running out of sand.

A child in another time shrieks, *Everybody, don't see me!*

stridently over & over. What will become of us

we wonder & search for each others' hands, closing

our fingers around one another like wild red poppies

clinging as we watch the indigo peaks fade.

There is a small deer at the edge of the copse

that has burrowed through the blackberry hedge

following a tunnel carved into the bramble wall

by many years of animals leading one another

to the ragged border of the cottonwoods, that maze

now winter bare behind the doe, who sniffs the water

laden atmosphere startling only slightly as a car sluices

past speeding on the wounded spine of asphalt

& she finds nothing new under the pewter sun,

just a humming, a dappling.

My mother swells like roses in her bell white gown,

turns on the bathroom light & never returns.

Bells ring in cathedrals & dells everywhere at once,

calling out the names of immense stones sawn in half,

ancestries etched in every single tone. As we watch her go,

no one calls out, calls her back, we do not dare startle

the veils, our breath like a sleds gliding so tenderly

over the air that opens the seams of the earth invisibly.

We hear a dog in the distance squeal in some sort of terror

or pain but we cannot reach out to comb its coat

gently with our palms. We have to hold on.

There seems no other way—or regret might gather

in a sea of black pebbles filling our throats & genitals.

Frozen, we bear witness as the indigo mountains

are carried away in the beaks of so many crows

like memories of something pure, truthful, until

the sky becomes a bed of spilled ink, a babbling roar,

drowning, not brave & costly like all true freedoms.

Goodbye we wave to the saturated peaks as the doe

comes to stand beside us staring at our locked hands,

then our wet feet covered in sticks & mud, then at our faces—

searching our eyes as if asking what color the future is,

asking like a fingerprint, or music, she studies, wearing

the same wordlessly quizzical look I'd last I seen my mother

wear when in the island house, she, in her white bell gown,

came to kneel with great pain at my side where I'd slept

on the floor near the fire & whispered, Did you do the right thing?

Do you still believe that's true? Then the kettle was screaming,

which simply meant it was time to go.

◆

AHUVA S. ZASLAVSKY

The Great Regression

Not again this mother father poem—
a snake game and I am never sure from which side
it will catch me off-guard

Picking up the pen feels like tracing myself limb after limb
And then repeat
Same pen. Should I write with my right side?
I promise myself not to write anymore mother/father poems

And I truly believe it is possible

but since this promise, it has been very hard
like when you are told not to think about a dangling camel
coming out from a mouth.
Can you really not think about it now?

So, I joke instead—
I call it "the poop and peepee poems"
Do you find it embarrassing? If you do, go ahead and you try,
or try not to write a poem about my mother and father
and tell me what is more pathetic

At least *pooppipi* makes me giggle

Speaking about poop, last night I dreamed
A big poop was coming out in public, like a good poem—soft, smooth
It was not embarrassing, nor did it smell
It looked like fresh chocolate clay

The crowd gathered around did not think it was shit at all
They thought it was beautiful

But to me, these people looked like the mass cheering for the naked emperor
I wanted to say: "Hey, you *are* looking at a pile of poop? Yeah?"
But the truth is
it felt good and came with a huge sense of accomplishment and relief

like the way a toddler feels the first time they succeed in poetry—
I mean—potty-training and their parents pop-in and peek in the pot
and cheer for me and I know I did something extraordinary
and don't really know what but I go with it

Now I think all this is really because I wanted to tell you about my dream
But again
poop and peepee and mothers and fathers and poetry
Do you find it embarrassing?

◆

BIRCH DWYER

Menopause

Earlier, the fire was bigger.
Standing out in the field at night you could see it
like a sun rising from the center of the forest, its light
illuminating the undersides of the trees.
But now, standing in that same field

all you see is a dark forest on a clouded night
and the eerie texture of trees.
You wonder if there is any fire left
to warm a cold night.

As you head towards the woods
and push through its outer layer,
you find a woman there, a part of you,
knelt down in the clearing.

She is bent over blowing embers,
her breath fanning fishtails of orange
and scarlet, purple green.
Her fire is close to the ground;

she leans in to warm her face
and the bones of her hands.
She is listening to wind talking to tree.
She is listening to earth thanking sky

and sky thanking earth, her calves kissing
the forest floor as a log collapses
and breaks open to reveal
embers and ash, trickles of fire.

◆

HOLADAY MASON

The Blue Dog

I dreamed I lost my blue dog.
My head was splitting under my Covid mask

like the round width of a tree, it's trunk cut
open by the axe of a faceless human,

the rings of years exposed & leaking
essentially the oily residue of every body's

story what is now & so very constantly,
the weight. One is taught not to

use words like *heart*, or *weep* or *dream*
in a poem—still I woke from the dream,

my heart weeping for the misplaced
hound—gleaming mutt plum sized

in my left palm—tiny hugging loving
free reign wolf, dog of kissing, touching,

hound of toothy grinning strangers
meeting in the street, shaking hands,

this wilder beast suddenly gone,
the scope & shape of its haunts

& hoods caged, tethered, lost
creature now heeling so close

to one's own bright black boots
it disappears as each heel smacks

rain slick pavement & I start running
nowhere, the day shining bright

as a coin flipped in the air
over a bet inevitably lost,

history rolling like dirty water
under bridges, & no cure, no home

for the blue mongrel I miss so bad
I fall & bleed just scrambling to catch it

& hold on tight before it fades again
like a child tucking between the walls

& the doors of a haunted house
or a city sparking through fog

or a meadow veiled in spring flora,
colors stinking damply before slipping away.

♦

GABBY HANCHER

how safety can feel like a frightened bird

that did not see the glass
a heart that beats frantically
as you lay there on domestic concrete
contrasted starkly by the liminal hours
when you think you are asleep
or in state of emergency

sweet one, dear one
surround this nightly grieving
with essential tenderness
wrap it up in feathered gauze
fragrant with lavender longing
until fragile bird bones
become air-born once more

until tender buds in right time
bloom through winter's frost

♦

ANDRA VLTAVÍN

Four Seasons of Hibernation

—After Ash Good & Beth Melnick

Here comes the *gnawing pressure*
to be supernatural in *a desert of unwillingness*
where the mermaids once braided

their hair and sang siren songs
of leaving the planet

for Neptune. I hope they made it there.
I whisper every longing I ever had
into sand, begging atoms

and molecules to make a reality
with less suffering than this one. Blow

from my hands a fine dust of wishes
or maybe bone. The garden
gave its last tomato, and the sun

aches toward liberation after a summer
that let no one out of their holes.

Always one more day until whatever
comes next in this inertial uncertainty,
but we stubbornly till ground again,

and wait for seed to sprout.

♦

awake

—After Julia Bray

no time / for sheep / name beings / who heal across futures / pasts / great distance / endless list certain / to defeat insomnia / do not count ones who believe / they are healers << *short list awake in the dark* / don't let it be some secret / we rely on cosmic back-up / what appears on time from some other place / I BELIEVE IN YOU << *do i need any other belief at all?* lapping ocean / YOU & YOU & YOU / *new dream* >> us / unshakable / sure / don't you hear the same song / we never mistake ourselves for imposters again

♦

ACKNOWLEDGMENTS

This anthology was edited & arranged by Ash Good & Andra Vltavín.

Gratitude to the editors of the following publications in which these poems first appeared, sometimes in different versions:

About Place—"421 Million Yards"

Cathexis Northwest Press—"us? beautiful / prepared for our own demise"

Clackamas Literary Review—"The Fledgling"

Hotel Amerika—"From the Mountains to The Prairies to The Oceans White With Foam"

Interlude (Pale Ale Poet Series 2001)—"A Long Dead Horse"

Not Very Quiet —"i haven't"

Rise Up Review —"but can novelty be our gender?"

Spillway—"Pulchritude"

The Weaver's Body (Tebot Press 2019)—"Spider"

Voicecatcher—"What It Is to Eat," "The Goose," "Menopause," and "Unexpected Conversation at Mid-life"

Windfall —"Basement Sink Communion"

On page 22 ("us? beautiful / prepared for our own demise") the lines "and this is all true," "for a while we live that revolution," "follow both of them in riot gear," "no stopping now i say" and "it hits me before it hits me" were drawn from workshop collaborators Andra Vltavín, Emily Dempsey and Rhonda Nichols.

Poets

SAMANTHA CIMINO (she/her) is an intuitive artist working with visual art, music, and movement. Her work explores mysticism, the feminine, a return to earth-based practices, and the birthright of free and playful expression. She is also an herbalist tending to emotional wellness and connection with nature and to the self.
@trinacreatura | @robesofdreams | www.samanthacimino.com

BIRCH DWYER is a writer and workshop facilitator living in Portland, Oregon. She currently leads Poetic Medicine circles through Portland Women Writers and for Transition Projects. Her writing has been published in *VoiceCatcher*, *Clackamas Literary Review* and *Windfall*. Birch makes her home with her husband and son and two dogs, one who likes to be rolled in a blanket like a burrito and the other who lies on the couch fully exposed, like an open-faced sandwich.

ASH GOOD is the author of several books of poetry. Their newest collection, *us clumsy gods,* is forthcoming from What Books Press in 2022. They are a queer, nonbinary and nonmonogamous poet, designer, curator and editor who centers liberation, play and movement while traveling the portal between outer- and inner-space. Ash is all about innovative narrative design, growth mindset, fresh sneakers, motorcycle road trips to national parks and fostering

rich collaborative spaces. They are cofounding editor at
First Matter Press and a reader for *Frontier Poetry* magazine.
Their poems appear in or are forthcoming from *Voicemail Poems,
Willawaw Journal, Cathexis Northwest Press, Not Very Quiet,
The Timberline Review, The Cape Rock, Rise Up Review* and others.
They live in Portland, Oregon (with uncountable noisy
houseplants). @justlightgrow | www.ashgood.com

GABBY HANCHER (they/she) is a queer creator and magic
maker from the Portland, OR. Her first chapbook of poems
is *The Growth Lines* (First Matter Press). As a writer, she mindfully
explores the intersection between trauma and resilience, calling
upon nature and childhood for illumination. The alchemy
of art and science is the crux of Gabby's playful light, seeking
to help others unite mind, body, and spirit in accessible,
compassionate ways. They are currently a counselor-in-training
with a special interest in the Hakomi method and attachment
work. Outside of writing, Gabby can be found dancing, enjoying
nature, and studying embodied social justice practices.
@a.tender.creature

JENN LALIME is a lover of story in all its forms. As a writer,
community builder, parent, partner, and friend, her life's work
is deepening her own voice and amplifying the voices of others.

While her love of travel has taken her across the globe, she is most at home in the forests of the Pacific Northwest. www.jennlalime.com

SIERRA VIDA LISA is a meaning-maker, video editor, avid karaoke enthusiast and emerging poet who has found immense healing in sharing sacred space with the writers in this circle. She didn't have the opportunity to go to school until high school, but she immediately loved English class. She loves with her whole heart and seeks to transform pain into healing along her cosmic journey. She's been called a human jukebox for the many song lyrics she can recite and often finds joy in puns, word play and rhymes. @sierraloveslife

HOLADAY MASON is the author of two chapbooks and five full-length collections—*Towards the Forest* & *Dissolve* (New Rivers Press), *The Red Bowl: A Fable in Poems* (Red Hen Press), *The "She" Series: A Venice Correspondence* with Sarah Maclay (What Books Press) and *The Weaver's Body* (Tebot Bach). Nominated for three Pushcarts, widely published, she is also a portrait and fine art photographer focusing on the beauty of aging and humans as a part of nature. A psychotherapist in private practice since 1986, Holaday also runs theraputic writing workshops that involve guided healing journeys into our inner worlds. She lives in Venice with the flocks of wild green parrots. @holadaymasonphotography | www.holadaymason.com

BETH MELNICK is committed to the practice of writing a short thing almost every day. She is a Reiki Master and photographer who has enjoyed a long, accidental career spanning over 25 years as a location scout and manager for film and still photography. This work has opened doors to other realities and intimately engaged her with people and situations she would never otherwise have known. Sometimes she writes about them. Beth lives with her husband and son in Portland, Oregon. @bethmelnick

DAWN THOMPSON oversees and facilitates writing workshops through Portland Women Writers, a writing collective fostering creativity, transformation, healing and connection. She is also the co-founder of Touchstone Retreats, which inspire transformation through art and story. Dawn holds writing circles through the Knight Cancer Institute at OHSU and Legacy Cancer Center for individuals healing from cancer. She believes writing our stories is a sacred act that liberates, heals and transforms us and that writing in community fosters connection and peace. When not in a writing circle, Dawn can be found in the natural world, competing in Masters Track & Field, dancing wild in her living room or spending time with her son, husband and the larger circle of her beloved family.
www.pdxwomenwriters.com

LUNITA VALERIA VELÁSQUEZ is a first generation American writer raised biculturally in Southern California near the Mexican border. She began writing poetry and short stories at an early age as an intrinsic medium to make sense of the world and the complexities of navigating humanness as a highly sensitive being. Her poetry has been shared through live readings, collaborative projects, independently curated zines, and digital publications over the years. Most recently, her writing has been deeply influenced by the exploration of authentic self expression, ancestral reclamation, elemental magick and dissent from the structures that confine our collective creative sovereignty. @lunitayoga | www.omlunita.org

ANDRA VLTAVÍN (formerly K. M. Lighthouse) is the author of *Body Until Light, Time Counts Backward from Infinity* and two chapbooks of poetry. The poet is very involved in activism and is learning how to create better systems for people to belong to than patriarchy, capitalism and white-body supremacy. They lead writing workshops; facilitate healing touch rituals; and believe that art, poetry and aesthetics are forms of divinity. They live the revolutions of queerness and polyamory and are very happily settled with a nesting partner, two bunnies and a spinning wheel at their home in Portland, Oregon. www.mermaidsinspace.com/andra

AHUVA S. ZASLAVSKY was born and raised in Tel Aviv, Israel and moved to Portland, Oregon in 2010. She graduated from The University of the Negev, Israel with a B.A in behavioral sciences. Ahuva is currently completing her MFA program at the Pacific Northwest College of Art in Visual Studies. In her work, she explores themes of memory in relation to trauma in cultural and domestic contexts, through different mediums—writing, painting, printing and sculpting. Her work has been shown in regional and national galleries including Alberta Abbey, Portland OR; Davidson Gallery, Seattle, WA; MGNE - Art Complex Museum, MA; Rhode Island Watercolor Society, and Crow's Shadow Institute of the Arts.
She has been a visiting artist at Crow's Shadow, OR and is currently a docent at The Jewish Museum in Portland, OR. www.ahuvasz.com

◆

www.ingramcontent.com/pod-product-compliance
Lightning Source LLC
Chambersburg PA
CBHW081159070526
44583CB00021B/2916